# The Oblivion Ha-Ha

# The Oblivion Ha-Ha

*Sixty Poems by*
JAMES TATE

Carnegie Mellon University Press
PITTSBURGH • 1997

Some of these poems have previously appeared in the following publications, to whose editors grateful acknowledgment is made: *The Atlantic, Atlantis* (Dublin), *Chicago Review, Choice, Cloud Marauder, Concerning Poetry, Fire Exit, Kayak, The Lace Curtain* (Dublin), *The New York Times, Poetry, Poetry Northwest, North American Review, The Poetry Bag, Lillabulero, Quarterly Review of Literature, Pym-Randall Press, Stony Brook Poetry Journal, Sumac, Suction, Tennessee Poetry Journal, Tri-Quarterly, Unicorn Journal,* and *Chelsea*. The poems "Coda" and "Shadowboxing" appeared originally in *The New Yorker*.

The author also wishes to thank the following publishers for permission to reprint poems which previously appeared in broadside, pamphlet or book: Black Sparrow Press, Kayak Press, Stone Wall Press and Unicorn Press.

Library of Congress Catalog Card No. 97-65566
ISBN 0-88748-215-5
Copyright © 1967, 1968, 1969, 1970 by James Tate
All rights reserved
Printed and bound in the United States of America

First Carnegie Mellon University Press Edition, October 1997

*The Oblivion Ha-Ha* was first published as An Atlantic Monthly Press Book by Little, Brown and Company, Boston, in 1970.

Publication of this book is supported by gifts to the Classic Contemporaries Series from James W. Hall, Richard M. Cyert, and other anonymous benefactors.

*For X* .

# Contents

### I

| | |
|---|---|
| Poem | 3 |
| Rape in the Engineering Building | 4 |
| The Blue Booby | 5 |
| The Day Lost | 7 |
| The Pet Deer | 8 |
| Cryptozoa | 9 |
| Plea Based on a Sentence from a Letter Received by the Indiana State Welfare Department | 10 |
| The Salute | 11 |
| Up Here | 12 |
| Applause for a Husband | 14 |
| Prose Poem | 16 |
| Dead-End Agenda | 17 |
| Coda | 18 |
| Cosmology | 19 |
| The Tryst | 20 |
| Pity Ascending with the Fog | 21 |
| The Coming Out of Ourselves Party | 22 |
| Little Yellow Leaf | 24 |
| Pride's Crossing | 25 |

### II

| | |
|---|---|
| Dark Street | 29 |
| The Indian Undertaker | 30 |

| | |
|---|---|
| A Pretty Girl Like That | 31 |
| Camping in the Valley | 32 |
| Peddler | 34 |
| The Tree Surgeon | 36 |
| The Answering Service | 38 |
| The Destination | 39 |
| Leaving Mother Waiting for Father | 40 |
| The Initiation | 41 |
| *Cecca Farfalla* | 42 |
| "The Whole World's Sadly Talking to Itself" | 43 |
| Consumed | 44 |
| Nativity | 45 |
| Shadowboxing | 46 |
| The Crushing Rose | 47 |
| Images of Little Compton, Rhode Island | 54 |
| From the Hole | 55 |
| The Trap | 56 |
| The Torches | 57 |
| The Plaza | 59 |
| Twilight Sustenance Hiatus | 60 |

## III

| | |
|---|---|
| The Wheelchair Butterfly | 63 |
| It's Not the Heat So Much as the Humidity | 65 |
| The Eagle Exterminating Company | 67 |
| The Arsonist as Benefactor | 68 |
| The Sleeper | 70 |
| The President Slumming | 71 |
| Vengeance | 72 |
| Jim's All Night Diner | 73 |
| Mrs. America | 74 |

| | |
|---|---|
| Scenario for Revolutionaries | 75 |
| Brotherhood/Shrouded Bridge | 77 |
| Stray Animals | 79 |
| When Kabir Died | 80 |
| Failed Tribute to the Stonemason of Tor House, Robinson Jeffers | 81 |
| Conjuring Roethke | 83 |
| Fire Dance | 85 |
| Dear Reader | 87 |
| No End to Fall River | 88 |
| Bennington | 89 |

# I

# Poem

High in Hollywood Hills a door opens:
a man disguised as a man appears,

sunglasses on his nose, a beard.
He can smell the flowers—camellia,
bougainvillea—the word,

itself a dream; the reality of the scene
was in the Chinese girl

who swam in the pool beneath
the rail he leaned on:
she was something else indeed.

She was the dream within
the dream within. He shouted: hallo,

halloo.
He did the handkerchief dance all alone.
O Desire! it is the beautiful dress

for which the proper occasion
never arises.

O the wedding cake and the good cigar!
O the souvenir ashtray!

# Rape in the Engineering Building

What I saw on his face scared me—ants
on jelly; two cars ducked as he zigzagged

past the library up to the tracks
where the other students were just falling

from classes. One big man yelled,
*stop him stop that man,* but I thought

it was personal and got out of their
way. Finally the aproned man told us

in a high stuck voice it was rape
in the engineering building, and

the rapist was chugging farther up
the inclined edge of town into

the shadowy upright garden.
Full of thanks, we took after him.

# The Blue Booby

The blue booby lives
on the bare rocks
of Galápagos
and fears nothing.
It is a simple life:
they live on fish,
and there are few predators.
Also, the males do not
make fools of themselves
chasing after the young
ladies. Rather,
they gather the blue
objects of the world
and construct from them

a nest—an occasional
Gaulois package,
a string of beads,
a piece of cloth from
a sailor's suit. This
replaces the need for
dazzling plumage;
in fact, in the past
fifty million years
the male has grown
considerably duller,
nor can he sing well.
The female, though,

asks little of him—
the blue satisfies her

completely, has
a magical effect
on her. When she returns
from her day of
gossip and shopping,
she sees he has found her
a new shred of blue foil:
for this she rewards him
with her dark body,
the stars turn slowly
in the blue foil beside them
like the eyes of a mild savior.

# The Day Lost

They would go riding through the woods of Tennessee
when they were first married: the gloaming green-
sward seduced their hearts, and they would stop to give
their weary steeds refreshment at a mountain spring.

Her high brown English boots were winning to his eye,
and she adored the parti-colored pants he wore.
The sun streamed through the leaves to make the trees
seem more like chandeliers. It was here he handed her

the ring; her tears flew, she was "at a loss for
words." On a silver anniversary in Indiana, she
stands in the north corner of the living room
in her negligee, snowshoes and skullcap, and he

is dancing on the table in his mackintosh and cummerbund.
Both realize how precious life is: to save time,
the horses are in the kitchen making soup.

# The Pet Deer

The Indian Princess
  in her apricot tea gown
moves through the courtyard
  teasing the pet deer

as if it were her lover.
  The deer, so small and
confused, slides on the marble
  as it rises on its hind legs

toward her, slowly, and with
  a sad, new understanding.
She does not know what
  the deer dreams or desires.

# Cryptozoa

I wish the stone lady would come to me.
Parakeet or no parakeet
the night is a vial of lighterfluid.
And I have been good, composing the perishable song
of my childhood: one dollar, one frond
meekly but loyally exploding the oath of circles.
I have been the best wound a diamond ever knew.

But what can I do for you? Write an encyclopedia
to which the least gnat could gain entrance?
I love you and I do not love you, perambulating utensils,
street names. An old man is giving mirrors
to a young girl. The meek have inherited the flypaper.
The past is more present than this moment.
I am drinking at a spring, my skin
is red and white. A little burning sensation,
a little joy I leave forever.

Oh well, I keep singing: I sing the song
of utensils, and there is one of street names,
and one of the names of dead pets.
The next day I am giving mirrors to a young girl.
I give free shoes for life to a stone lady.
She walks on air, she walks near the earth
in a region called the cryptosphere.

# Plea Based on a Sentence from a Letter Received by the Indiana State Welfare Department

Like lemon jello in a dream-
child's hand, here is my heart,

I don't know what to do with it

anymore, now that you are dead
certain there is no chance
for me to improve my state
of mind. Virginia, I have been
sitting here for three months

wringing my hands, nodding
my head, swaying, my whole body

swaying in ignorance.
Could you come over? I happen
to know you're miserable.
Could we hide the bones

of the past and apply rouge
to the cheeks of the future?

I will make you more attractive
than you could make yourself.
I am forwarding my marriage

certificate and six children;
I have seven but one died

which was baptized on half
a sheet of paper . . .

## The Salute

I dreamed a black widow dream all night.
Her legs were as long
and velvet as a debutante's.

She was my only friend,
and the little language she spoke
I completely misunderstood.

So full of poison she was,
my heart poured out to her.
She kissed me!

I was thrilled, my stiff body swooned
like a dead orchid,
and also like a rose I blushed.

She slapped her knobby knees
and ran away. I salute
this lady with obedient white fingers

for she is a widow by choice,
and I her mate.

## Up Here

The motel was made for love
as you were. I undressed you
with grace and tenderness,
kissing each newly bared part.

There you lay, your small, white
body throbbing in my hand
like a bird. We were silent.
The right word was not needed.

*Supple.* What was I doing
suddenly pacing around
the bed, scratching my head,
staring down at your gaze up
at me? *Recognition.*

I would not call you *svelte.*
Your breasts were barely a hand-
ful; I like small breasts, which fit
a hand. Your thighs were a feast,
though, and, walking, now and then
I would dip down to nibble
them. They were good: *wholesome.*
They were the bread of life.

Now your lips are moving, now
your hands reach up at me.
I feel as if I might be one
or two thousand feet above you.
Your lips form something, a bubble,

which rises and rises into
my hand: inside it is a word:
*Help.* I would like to help,
believe me, but up here nothing
is possible, nothing is clear:
*Help. Help me.*

## Applause for a Husband

Your own little banshees
with bare behinds
up before dawn
and in the cupboards
egg yolks between
pages of
invaluable documents

the wife sleeping
later and the martini
perfume
like a halo
over her face
and the eye-
liner across the pillow

like an old country road
her o goddamn
headache wringing
an apology
from you as if
you had made her
drink one more

before sending
the boys home
the boys not wanting

to go home
there being one more act
one costume
still to adorn

one breast rising
from the scooped
line
like a dove
and fluttering
for the poor
drunk boys who

do not know
how to leave
at this point
who have such
*respect*
for you
but who cannot believe

your love
will not expand
to include
their breathings
their applause
fills your heart
like a mortar shell

you gloat over it
you are one
of the blessèd.

## Prose Poem

I am surrounded by the pieces of this huge
puzzle: here's a piece I call my wife, and
here's an odd one I call convictions, here's
conventions, here's collisions, conflagrations,
congratulations. Such a puzzle this is! I
like to grease up all the pieces and pile
them in the center of the basement after
everyone else is asleep. Then I leap head-
first like a diver into the wretched confusion.
I kick like hell and strangle a few pieces,
bite them, spitting and snarling like a mongoose.
When I wake up in the morning, it's all fixed!
My wife says she would not be caught dead at
that savage resurrection. I say she would.

# Dead-End Agenda

Going by a thousand mailboxes soon
    going by a glass fountain
where a glass hand will touch my shoulder
Watching the calendar burn through the night
    getting my name changed
I'll be celebrating my new freedom
with the hangman in an elevator

I'll be listening to a muffled drum
    huddled in a corner
with two camels and a glass of vodka
    crossing a fjord
    climbing six flights of stairs
    walking on eggshells
        sorry I ever left you . . .

# Coda

Love is not worth so much;
I regret everything.
Now on our backs
in Fayetteville, Arkansas,
the stars are falling
into our cracked eyes.

With my good arm
I reach for the sky,
and let the air out of the moon.
It goes whizzing off
to shrivel and sink
in the ocean.

You cannot weep;
I cannot do anything
that once held an ounce
of meaning for us.
I cover you
with pine needles.

When morning comes,
I will build a cathedral
around our bodies.
And the crickets,
who sing with their knees,
will come there
in the night to be sad,
when they can sing no more.

# Cosmology

The animals in hiding
we live on what they discard
a lady's rib cage
(stuffed with maggots but good)

magazines, the sun.
In your dream we never saw each other again.

In mine worlds collide.

# The Tryst

In the early evening rain
I leave the vault
and walk into the city

of lamentations, and stand.
I think it is September, September.

Where are you Josephine?
It is one minute until you must appear,
draped in a grass-green serape,

shorter than most people,
more beautiful, baleful . . .

pressing a hand to my forehead,
slipping into my famished pocket
the elixir, the silver needle.

# Pity Ascending with the Fog

He had no past and he certainly
had no future. All the important
events were ending shortly before
they began. He says he told mama

earth what he would not accept: and I
keep thinking it had something to do
with her world. Nights expanding into
enormous parachutes of fire, his

eyes were little more than mercury.
Or sky-diving in the rain when there
was obviously no land beneath,
half-dead fish surfacing all over

his body. He knew all this too well.
And she who might at any time be
saying the word that would embrace all
he had let go, he let go of course.

I think the pain for him will end in
May or January, though the weather
is far too clear for me to think of
anything but august comedy.

# The Coming Out of Ourselves Party

You wanted to be strong.
I wanted to congratulate all of us
on giving in.
Gum wrappers are wriggling in the sun.
Mrs. Mendosa's voice rattles
around Jefferson Street two times,
and ends spinning
like a BB in a can.

Then I thought of all the women
I had ever had. I appreciate
the patronage; thanks for dropping in.
But the King relinquishes his zither.

We were last together
at The Colonial Inn, in Concord, Massachusetts.
We had a free television;
we were allowed to park without charge,
and given a direct dial telephone;
sixty air-conditioned rooms,
including The Thoreau Room,
The Emerson Bar and The Hawthorne John.
You wanted to have integrity.
What a day, the clerk said.

The sky is disheveling overhead.
The pulse of the earth is slowing.

On this street, there is not even a radio.
The days continue to eat each other;
the doors grow little and thick.
Always, finally, we are untouched.

This was to be the coming out of ourselves party,
to which we had all looked forward.
This was to be bigger than life;
this, the inside story.

## Little Yellow Leaf

A woman's pink body could be preserved
separate from the mass and the mill.
An anonymous though urgent love capable
of disassembling the rest of us
like a pure white puzzle of an essay
fraught with hyphens. Preserved forever
inside a glacier she moves across
the valley like a violin: our gladness
flares like a pheasant in an empty field.

How strong the need to comprehend
the little lights and bells inside
our heads when she slides by!
Avalanches will begin soon and maybe
flood the town below. I think I know
her name, her name is Little Yellow Leaf:
I should not let the others know.
She is deathless dream: she holds
loose and spare parts of lost loves

together with one slender, revolving
finger. The world needs a love
it cannot buy or chain: untouchable,
Little Yellow Leaf, lure us beyond
loss and gain. Let profit be
the love we part with, and failure
the first day of the rest of our lives.

## Pride's Crossing

Where the railroad meets the sea,
I recognize her hand.
Where the railroad meets the sea,
her hair is as intricate as a thumbprint.
Where the railroad meets the sea,
her name is the threshold of sleep.

Where the railroad meets the sea,
it takes all night to get there.
Where the railroad meets the sea,
you have stepped over the barrier.
Where the railroad meets the sea,
you will understand afterwards.

Where the railroad meets the sea,
where the railroad meets the sea—
I know only that our paths lie together,
and you cannot endure if you remain alone.

II

## Dark Street

So this is the dark street
where only an angel lives:
I never saw anything like it.
For the first time in a lifetime
I feel the burgeoning of wings
somewhere behind my frontal lobes.
So this is the dark street.
Did his lights come on,
or do I dream?
I never saw anything like it.

Even the trees' languorous leaves
look easy to touch.
So this is the dark street.
Here he comes now:
good afternoon, Father—
your handshake is so pleasing.
Brush the shards from my shoulders,
what lives we have ahead of us!
So this is the dark street.
I never saw anything like it.

# The Indian Undertaker

There is a man carrying an armload of lilacs
across the field: he may be a lost Indian
as he is whistling, very beautifully, a tune
to the birds I have never heard. I am in back
of him, following at a distance. Three small quail,
perhaps hypnotized, rise and circle his head.
I want to stop the man and ask him what he said
to make them feel so safe, but I feel
weak and dizzy. His whistling begins to chill
my neck, as if the wind from his lips were
rushing round me. If only I were agile
like this family of field mice heading for
the river; still, I am not sorry I came here.

A lilac is falling like a piece of sky
from his arms; it seems to take ten minutes or more.
Finally it kisses the wet earth. I
start running—the lilac is waiting for me.
Here you are! I feel the first emotions of love.
And, look, a snail is holding on to your leaf
for all he's worth. So slowly he moves,
humming a psalm to the god of snails.
The lilac swoons. The ground is sapphire
and the trees are topaz. I feel as if I were
attending my own funeral, the air a jail
of music and cool yellow fire.

## A Pretty Girl Like That

Now in a shabby raincoat
along the pier, now her flaming hair;
her blood is a noise
and makes the window tremble.

Her movement is bewildered desire,
she has no coverings for her eyes:
now a dry hand rockets forth,
and dies. She might never

be seen again: aquamarine lies,
damned aria—she holds
her black gloves as if the sea
had just proffered them.

Is she drunk or is she asleep?
Thrilling loons cry
in the cloudless air.
There is no answer anywhere.

# Camping in the Valley

Here is a place for my gun.
I need everything less and less,
have you noticed?
But I feel something, almost

anything is having some effect
on me. I think I believe
what I'm saying.
Are you having a little trouble

keeping up, dear?
Now I am ready to survive,
though I suppose we are in danger
sitting here, arms crossed,

in the valley
with the black pig on the spit,
our little doggy.
I have faith the air will

soon cohere or speak,
tomorrow morning as you are
pulling on your boots,
my love, by the fire.

I can't see what the blue mosses
are doing now, dripping
from the bridge I'd guess.
The toads beneath travel home

through the sprung doors
of the river;
on either side of myself
the water is seldom

so navigable. Yes, it behooves us
to close our eyelids again,
the cold front, the rain,
the sun rising around 5:17,

an important mission in the morning:
what was it? The juniper berries?
The death we thought we left
in the mountains like a child.

# Peddler

Please do not steal my flowers;
they are my last love,
I am immune to everything

but flowers. The pageantry
of most encounters
is not quite as exciting

as the pollinating
pasqueflower, it's like a river
washing itself over

and over.
And when the pretty waitress
Lillian of French descent

walks over a grate in the sidewalk
and a gush of hot air
slams her dress over her ears

I do not enjoy the view
as much as that of phlox blooming.
I regard human beings as signals

and therefore bow my head
to hide my silly grin
at the raucous world—a monkey

hanging by its tail
from an intensely white cliff:
that's why we hold out

our hands all day, all life,
to catch something like that.
And nightletters, the urgent hundred

syllables by which we
express less than the minimal
Aristotelian tragedy—

an ash to swallow every morning
with my cereal,
a dictionary of stones in the evergreen.

In the distance the man
who is in charge of beating children
hangs his hands on my cart

and I sprinkle pollen of goldenrod
on his open wounds:
these are ordinary obligations,

but flowers, flowers—
there are so many colors;
more than there were

in poor Joseph's coat I think.

# The Tree Surgeon

All limbs are not necessary:
I have a tree surgeon in mind.
He is such a lonely man,
but he is kind,
and the tree is in need

of his gentle hands.
Not all limbs are necessary,
my wife agrees.
She is a cripple from the Bronx;

something about a train
in Yucatan . . .

or the way she talks
makes me think
you're better off
hobbling in the dark—

the thieves offer you their staffs.
The willow like an octopus
in the moon

knots its arms
on whose behalf? The surgeon
is broke; inflammable trucks
drive round his flat,

the drivers honk
at his long, green and gray hands.
His life is stained

with the breath
of an idle neighborhood,
like a window on a bus.
A number of limbs fall on the dogs.

# The Answering Service

Brother, the telephone
is ringing in the field:

we are occupied
Intelligence quotient,

none. Over
your peculiar will

we have knitted a cape.
A meteor, a burst

of stars put out.
The sluggish goon

left in the corner—
preposterous

to think of him.
Sterile or queer,

gorging himself
on sherbet, his shoulders

on his knees;
or venturing a paper

airplane. Uneven
movements as he rises

to answer
the telephone ringing

for one of us
in the black bean field.

# The Destination

All day red hatpins fall out
of the sky, so I fasten
myself to a tree and let
the velvet and light inside

of it love and comfort me:
could this be the way life ends?
I carry away the tree,
place it in my car and start

toward home, not feeling a part
of anything anymore;
thinking, I don't want to live
in this place twice, I jam on

the brakes and clear my throat
of human hair, climb out of
the car, stare at the junkman
staring into the flames

of the tree—goodbye, little friend.
I walk to Seattle, sell
my old clothes, sleep alone all
week in a park on the ground,

wake to find my head dropping
visions of six children
ripping open a reindeer.
I am sad and befuddled,

going the direction I think
is worst, with papers tied to
my ankles, wondering if
this is the way life begins.

# Leaving Mother Waiting for Father

The evening went on;
I got very old.
She kept telling me it didn't matter.
The real man would come back
soon. We waited. We had alarms
fixed, vases of white and purple
flowers ready to thrust
on him should he.

We had to sell the place
in a hurry; walked downtown
holding hands.
She had a yard of blue material in her pocket:
I remember that so well!
She fell asleep and a smile
began to blister her old mouth.
I propped her against a hotel
and left without any noise.

## The Initiation

The long wake continues,
quiet and moronic expressions.
The jowl of the dead
is agape with infinite abandon
as if he were about to sing:
if we concentrate
he may remember the words.

In comes a man with a dog
on a chain; then several others.
The room is bathed
in plaster of paris.
In the background
a deep, abundant fugue has begun
The piece is dedicated
to me. How strange,
I thought I was new here.

They stop playing,
file quickly into another room.
As I begin to leave
shafts of darkness reach out
and close the little door.

# Cecca Farfalla

You are seated in the delicatessen,
eating a Polish sausage;
there is an austere butterfly

on the end of your nose,
it blinds you. There may be
something voluptuously
worthwhile on the other side;

through a veil you step,
skin very taut,
beyond the green trolley,

the horns, the burning sausage.
There are human beings near.
You are not thankful. The light—

no, not trying to get out,
not wiggling, gasping,
just standing in thick traffic.

She of the long dress
and gray hair saves you, and says:
Spring has brought you back to us.
You can't hear,
you lean but you cannot.

There is a blind butterfly in your ear.
It is *farfalla*, she whispers, in Italian.

## "The Whole World's Sadly Talking to Itself"

Hands full of sand, I say:
take this, this is what I have saved;
I earned this with my genius,
and because I love you . . .

take this, hurry.
I am dropping everything.
And then I listened:
I was not saying anything;
out of all that had gone into
the composition of the language
and what I knew of it
I had chosen these words—
take this, hurry—
and you could not hear me.
I had said nothing
And then I am leaving,

making ready to go to another street
when you, mingled between
sleep and delirium, turned

and handed me an empty sack:
take this, friend,
I am not coming back. The ghost
of a flower poised on your lip.

# Consumed

Why should you believe in magic,
pretend an interest in astrology
or the tarot? Truth is, you are

free, and what might happen to you
today, nobody knows. And your
personality may undergo a radical

transformation in the next half
hour. So it goes. You are consumed
by your faith in justice, your

hope for a better day, the rightness
of fate, the dreams, the lies
the taunts.—Nobody gets what he

wants. A dark star passes through
you on your way home from
the grocery: never again are you

the same—an experience which is
impossible to forget, impossible
to share. The longing to be pure

is over. You are the stranger
who gets stranger by the hour.

# Nativity

Only his skull and his testicles were found
in a shadowbox which receded as you approached.
There was a sound in infinity which went something like this:

the tractor drove through a field of snakes
a nativity of abiding darkness
nothing serious

# Shadowboxing

Sometimes you almost get a punch in.
Then you may go for days without even seeing him,
or his presence may become a comfort
for a while.

He says: I saw you scrambling last night
on your knees and hands.

He says: How come you always want to be
something else, how come you never take your life
seriously?

And you say: Shut up! Isn't it enough
I say I love you, I give you everything!

He moves across the room with his hand
on his chin, and says: How great you are!

Come here, let me touch you, you say.

He comes closer. Come closer, you say.
He comes closer. Then. *Whack!* And
you start again, moving around and around
the room, the room which grows larger
and larger, darker and darker. The black moon.

# The Crushing Rose

I
You must be the fool
When they say you are guilty
say innocent and when
they say innocent
demand guilt
When you hunt the elephant

take a feather
Tell the doctor it doesn't hurt
except when he kisses it
You are lost in your own house
The drawer full of light
bulbs is locked and the key

is in Florida
attached to a kite
What you invent each night
is the mystery of life
You tell the wrong man
and he hangs you

with your own hands
You can't die though
the world needs you
Out of hunger
and chaos a tired voice
calls for a donkey

and you know he means you.

II

They exist almost always
on a bed of roses and
frequently dance the fox-trot.
At night they listen to the bread
in the cupboard sigh. A nail
is like a requiem!

Then there is the need
to destroy a bird's nest.
O the poor blinded flies,
all they can do is wrangle
with pigs about the quality
of oranges. In life,

never do as others do.

III

Though the odds were in your favor
the figure in the doorway
has chosen you, an expedient conclusion
to the strife of evil, a raid

on glad tidings. How do you
maneuver now with the recurring dream
of love fleeing toward meaning-
lessness like a white deer?

The dark is an available religion.
Come forward and kneel before
your television. There are the airplanes
with folded wings, there is the snow

which comes down on us like a shadow.
Everyone wins a prize in the theater
of the crushing rose.
I would as lief have loved you.

IV

Nothing is what it seems:
for instance, these legumes, beans.
I certainly do not know
what it all means, the alterations
occurring to my pants' leg
in the middle of the night.
The candle that follows me

through the downtown diner.
I could cry. An Eric Satie sweatshirt
delivered anonymously.
An address book that can kiss
exactly as you like to.
Should one call the police
and report the stolen thief's ring.
It hurts. It stings.

My books are melting, they are the first
and last ingredients
of the terrible birthday soup.
All night I stand outside my window
and watch myself sleep.
He knew better. The coffee needed him.
So what. There are stones to read,

trees to zipper. There is the wren
forever on the sill I must croon to.
It makes me nervous. The thing gets done.
The telephone book is memorized,

I am encouraged to swallow
the Scotch tape. Which
has nothing to do with *bliss*.

If you do not understand that
an execution of the toy heart
must follow. As you say, business
is business. I only write the damned things
for you to bleed them.

V

We were so hungry
we collapsed under
the spiraea.
A couple of fierce hounds
examined us,

we spoke their language,

it just came to us
They said to be patient,
a big surprise
was on its way.
The white one put his foot
by mistake

in the water.
The brown one thought this
a great joke, laughed
and laughed and finally
fell over the cliff.
The white one said

the only surprise
was the last one, though
a red dog
in the center of the bush
violently disagreed.
All the time

we were quietly dying.
We did not speak
the language
of the squirrels, though.
We thought
it was funny.

## VI

The sail was torn to ribbons
and a bug kept hitting me in the eye.
We had one piece of toast between us.
We thought we should try to signal;
I made a kind of flag
out of her blouse. How long

could we go on floating that way,
the iris view toward dusk
was a soft thorn to our rue.
On her finger she balanced a pill:
It was the fatal toilet
of understanding. It had been

nibbled at—she had no right
to row with her hair.

# Images of Little Compton, Rhode Island

Here the tendons in the swans' wings stretch,
feel the tautness of their futuristic necks,
imagine their brains' keyhole accuracy,
envy their infinitely precise desires.

A red-nosed Goodyear zeppelin emerges from the mist
like an ethereal albino whale on drugs.

One wanders around a credible hushed town.

Mosquito hammering through the air
with a horse's power: there will be no cameramen.
We will swap bodies maybe
giving the old one a shove.

That's an awful lot of work for you I said
and besides look at your hands,
there are small fires in the palms,
there is smoke squirting from every pore.

O when all is lost,
when we have thrown our shoes in the sea,
when our watches have crawled off into weeds,
our typewriters have finally spelled perhaps
accidentally the unthinkable word,

when the rocks loosen and the sea anemones
welcome us home with their gossamer arms
dropping like a ship from the stars,

what on earth shall we speak or think of,
and who do you think you are?

# From the Hole

A horse-drawn rocket
climbs the wooden hill:
behind it two or three friends
are sharing their tobacco: their hats
are beautiful like small pieces of
coal on their heads
fostering goodwill.
I'm standing in this hole, see,
and I'm going to holler out:
"Good riddance to bad rubbish!"
and "I'm sorry if I was a menace!"
"Howdy doody, milkman travail!"
"So long buoys and grills."
Like a harp
burning on an island
nobody knows about.

# The Trap

Inside the old chair
I found another chair;
though smaller, I liked
sitting in it better.
Inside that chair
I found another chair;
though smaller, in
many ways I felt
good sitting in it.
Inside that chair
I found another chair;
it was smaller and
seemed to be made
just for me.
Inside that chair,
still another;
it was very small,
so small I could
hardly get out of it.
Inside that chair
I found yet another;
and in that, another,
and another, until
I was sitting in
a chair so small
it would be difficult
to say I was sitting
in a chair at all.
I could not rise
or fall, and no one
could catch me.

# The Torches

How can I report the weariness
There was none
There was only a voice
which chanted its nonsense

over and over until
we were certain we understood
In blackness we rose
loading a few essential items

There were small villages
of starlight in the trees
hats and jewelry
Our boots barely touched the ground

We were experienced hikers
Rabbits and turtles disappeared
Leaves and twigs never broke
Some of the old fathers fell

and had to be carried
Their body rags had an odor
which was not pleasing
but to be pleased

was not our desire
At last we reached the cliff
even in the darkness
we could see for miles and miles

Glances were exchanged
and we hurled our torches
like babies into the river
each weeping louder than the other

A few sparks hung in the wind
and drifted back into our faces
so we turned and started back
down the path toward home

When we arrived it was morning
The neighborhood was doing
what it had to do
papers and milk and mail

We were surprised to find
that it had not changed
or if in fact there was a great change
suddenly we cared.

## The Plaza

The ubiquitous silver lights
throb on the Russian olive

trees; behold the penciling
of these yellow and blue

nativities; and the peacock
voices . . . and now the snow

descending on a little aqua-
marine wings into the heart

of our dark rejoicing
prehistoric city!

# Twilight Sustenance Hiatus

The relentless confetti of dollars!
I'd prefer to kiss that silent chipmunk
on the roadside while a tiny ocean
of dandelion seeds arranges a gray
throne on his ear! I have no "final"
vows to take tonight, though your hair
might be floating down the Ohio.
Chameleons can march around a small room
if they want. I could sell gasoline

on the desert, though I would miss
the grass. Or I could even get your name
tattooed gingerly across my wrist at dawn.
There is so little news fit to print:
yesterday a moth caught fire.
Today a lost school of astronomers
came back. We only think tomorrow
is called "The Finished Gem."
Tomorrow is called . . . come on.

III

# The Wheelchair Butterfly

O sleepy city of reeling wheelchairs
where a mouse can commit suicide if he can

concentrate long enough
on the history book of rodents
in this underground town

of electrical wheelchairs!
The girl who is always pregnant and bruised
like a pear

rides her many-stickered bicycle
backward up the staircase
of the abandoned trolleybarn.

Yesterday was warm. Today a butterfly froze
in midair; and was plucked like a grape
by a child who swore he could take care

of it. O confident city where
the seeds of poppies pass for carfare,

where the ordinary hornets in a human's heart
may slumber and snore, where bifocals bulge

in an orange garage of daydreams,
we wait in our loose attics for a new season

as if for an ice-cream truck.
An Indian pony crosses the plains

whispering Sanskrit prayers to a crater of fleas.
Honeysuckle says: I thought I could swim.

The Mayor is urinating on the wrong side
of the street! A dandelion sends off sparks:
beware your hair is locked!

Beware the trumpet wants a glass of water!
Beware a velvet tabernacle!

Beware the Warden of Light has married
an old piece of string!

## It's Not the Heat
## So Much as the Humidity

Only a dish of blueberries could pull me
out of this lingering funk.
I'm tired of taking the kids down
to watch the riot, no longer impressed
with fancy electrical nets, sick
of supersonic nightsticks.

Buy myself a hot dog and a glass of beer—
that helps. It's hard to say
who's winning. Nobody is winning.

Boy, Kansas City! Big Zoo! Oriental art!
Starlight Theater: *Annie Get Your Gun*
going into its seventeenth year.
Once I met Tab Hunter there, four o'clock
in the morning, standing in line

at the Coke machine, so tall and blond,
though not much of a conversationalist.

It's good to be home, trying to soften
the blow for young girls who are inclined
to fall off their porches.

Some of my best friends are . . .
Curse on those who do or do not take dope.

When Autumn comes, O when Fall arrives,
in her chemise of zillion colors,

I will sigh noisily, as if an old and
disgusting leg had finally dropped off.

No more drinking beer, no more
the perpetual search for an air-
conditioned friend, no more friends.

I'll take piano lessons, French lessons,
speed-reading lessons, and if there is
still time to kill, gawk at a bluejay
tumbling out of the maple tree.

Cars slide by with their windows up,
whispering of a Mexican Restaurant
"with really good Chili Verde."

The gutters billow with mauve death;
a mother's sad voice sends out
a tugboat whistle through the purple mist:
she worries about her children.

And the dangerous fishhook of melancholy
dangles from every dog's ear.
The dog that saved my life,
that keeps on saving it each long, humid night.
The dead dog. And so:

a shiny baseball hovers over the city.
No one asks why. And so: it passes on.
And so: a telephone starts to ring
in a widow's cake-filled kitchen . . .

A rollerskate collides with a lunchpail.

# The Eagle Exterminating Company

There are birds larger than us, I know that.
There is a bird in the bedroom much larger than the bed.
There is a photograph of a dead bird somewhere,
    I can't remember.
There is a wingspan that would put us all in the shadows.

There is the birdcall I must anticipate each night.
There are feathers everywhere.
Everywhere you walk there are feathers, you can try
to hop over and between them but then
you look like a bird. You are too small to be one.

You look like a tiny one-winged bird.
If you are your mother will come and kill you.
If you are not you will probably beat yourself to death.

But what matters is that every room in the house is filled,
is filled with the cry of the eagle.
Exterminating the eagles is now all but impossible
for the house would fall down without them.

There is a photograph of a dead bird somewhere.
Everywhere you walk there are feathers.
You look like a tiny one-winged bird.
There is the birdcall. There is the wingspan.

## The Arsonist as Benefactor

In this alien gray leg of Boston
even the commercial clairvoyants
have failed to find me. So what

have I accomplished, even if I
have forgotten where I lived
before, for what dubious though

incorrigible end, and the degree
to which I succeeded? An arsonist?
I don't know; I remember flames

five stories high with human
breath and fingers that comforted
me some years ago, gave me

the Season's spirit; and museums
crammed with the dregs of
inconsolable men, firing; and

the night I controlled a governor's
bituminous sleep so easily . . .
So many nights illumined by

my ill desires. But I'm not certain
of this. There is a chance that
I was innocent, an ordinary fire-

man with a deck of cards handy,
plenty of wax, listlessly alive
in some Pavlovian way. Or perhaps

I've always been right here,
everybody's and anything's sentinel.
I am tonight especially careful.

I watch graceful marlins
leap and feed in the arteries
of Puerto Rican children.

Then comes their obese mama
with a ton of groceries in each
double arm, swearing in a couple

of languages. As she herds them
toward the door, I calculate
that the tenement is blazing

inside, and that the mystery of
their survival is about to be solved.
But what can I say? How can I

explain? Sweetness, you deserve
more, but as your only benefactor,
if this will help you go, I pray

for nothing but your radiance.

## The Sleeper

Long white hairs knot his fingers
which have grown into his chest like snakes.
His feet grip each other like Gila monsters.
There are toads in his ears,
boulders in his blood.
His house is floating, gasping, exploding
under the ocean of his children
who flee on insane ladders
into the dark university.

## The President Slumming

In a weird, forlorn voice
he cries: it is a mirage!
Then tosses a wreath of scorpions
to the children,
mounts his white nag
and creeps off into darkness,
smoking an orange.

## Vengeance

A man is dripping blood
onto the snow-topped lawn,

and we are furious
because the cold has split

our tongues. We make hissing
sounds, *ssspt! ssspt!*

And we ignore him.
If only the sun would come

we could go to the beach,
snapping each other with towels—

mauve welts would be seen
rising! After a while they

would grow smaller until
our eyes would strain

to see the color,
a trail of rubies in the snow,

where is he going so slowly?

# Jim's All Night Diner

They wait as if for a certain invitation.
One desires to touch their lowly shoulders
and change them into green rabbits

on a white Alpine mountain,
their gauzy faces exhilarated
with a blue spray.
You find yourself instead

with a toy harpoon,
lurching fearfully at the evil rose
of poverty. Then you leave and,
walking through lush black woods,

imagine you have seen the world,
the very real world,
or a small jade buddha

falling from a red cloud.

## Mrs. America

She rearranges the furniture
so that it might resemble the beauty
of the saliva on the lip of the slave
when he thinks of her

carrying her portfolio through the fog
and into his cottage, beret askew,
lifebuoy cradled between her knees.

When the lamp barks she's obligated
to play the flute as if she were
an American Negro at a cakewalk
twenty or thirty years ago.

A lizard runs up and down her leg
so she guesses it must be the breeze.

Her children kneel at her feet
and taunt her with black flowers.

The silent cameras of hemophilia
have recorded all this a thousand times:
we bury her and then dig her up.

We bury her and then dig her up.
We would do anything for her.
You cannot imagine what we would do.

# Scenario for Revolutionaries

The wooden key in a stone hand.
Tigers turning down side alleys

in waves; huge nervous shapes,
looming over a still victim,

prick the air with claws.
Rolling up hills where small men

and women are arguing in a row
of blue houses. Or curl around

the legs of a girl running
to catch a bus, penetrate the coat

of an icy man, cudgel a stopsign.
Fog under the automobile accident

unfolds like an electric blanket.
It slows down life for a moment.

Then the knives, guns and chains
are delivered. Shining, they are

as beautiful as baby spoons.
The unknown mouth of death flashes

in a water-filled cave, a gigantic
orange wound that never heals

and is constantly churning.
Brown mice scuttle like soft

flexible jeeps out of the pine trees
in the dark beside the road

which bled. The subtle lapping
sounds which sound like a rocking

washbasin, but are the placenta
of the north registering the stirrings

of the infant Paul Bunyan.
Then we hesitantly slay the daughters

of the daughters of the DAR
whose flag is made of old veins.

Seeking our fullness, we are those
who suffer toward eternity

with a marble eye,
the insect of sleep gone forever.

# Brotherhood/Shrouded Bridge

They say it
is the longest bridge
in the world, also the cable
wire alone
would encircle
the earth almost three
times. I am afraid!

It cost almost eighty
million dollars.
I'll take it!
Six lanes for automobile
traffic on the upper
deck, and three
lanes for trucks and

buses, plus two
interurban tracks—
what does that mean?—
on the lower deck.
Today "smog" shrouded
much of it; one could
not see beyond

the first two truss
spans—there are
*many*. The bridge was
severed in space!
We keep going—fall

together, flounder among
freighters together,

or glide down onto
Treasure Island, which
is the largest man-made
island in the world:
eleven dredges were used
to complete operations
from which four-hundred

acres of level land
resulted. The last enemy
that shall be destroyed
is death: What did you
say your name was,
friend, I have been
thinking of . . .

## Stray Animals

This is the beauty of being alone
toward the end of summer:
a dozen stray animals asleep on the porch
in the shade of my feet,
and the smell of leaves burning
in another neighborhood.
It is late morning,
and my forehead is alive with shadows,
some bats rock back and forth
to the rhythm of my humming,
the mimosa flutters with bees.
This is a house of unwritten poems,
this is where I am unborn.

# When Kabir Died

They fought over his body.
The Mohammedans wanted to bury

the remains, while the Hindus
desired to burn them.

They argued so for days.
Then Kabir appeared before them!

and told them to go
to the casket and remove his

shroud. Both parties obeyed.
They found, in place

of the corpse, a heap
of flowers, half of which were

taken to Maghar by
the Mohammedans and buried,

the other half to Benares
and burned by the Hindus.

As Kabir himself has said,
we can reach the goal

without crossing the road.
Or, no: at the heart

of the Universe, white
music is blossoming.

# Failed Tribute to the Stonemason of Tor House, Robinson Jeffers

We traveled down to see your house,
Tor House, Hawk Tower, in Carmel,
California. It was not quite what
I thought it would be: I wanted it
to be on a hill, with a view of the ocean
unobstructed by other dwellings.
Fifty years ago I know you had
a clean walk to the sea, hopping
from boulder to boulder, the various
seafowl rightly impressed with
your lean, stern face. But today

with our cameras cocked we had to
sneak and crawl through trimmed lawns
to even verify the identity of
your strange carbuncular creation,
now rented to trillionaire non-
literary folk from Pasadena.
Edged in on all sides by trilevel
pasteboard phantasms, it took
a pair of good glasses to barely see
some newlyweds feed popcorn
to an albatross. Man *is*

a puny thing, divorced,
whether he knows it or not, and
pays his monthly alimony,
his child-support. Year after year
you strolled down to this exceptionally
violent shore and chose your boulder;

the arms grew as the house grew
as the mind grew to exist outside
of time, beyond the dalliance
of your fellows. Today I hate
Carmel: I seek libation in the Tiki

Bar: naked native ladies are painted
in iridescent orange on velvet cloth:
the whole town loves art.
And I donate this Singapore Sling
to the memory of it, and join
the stream of idlers simmering outside.
Much as hawks circled your head
when you cut stone all afternoon,
kids with funny hats on motorscooters
keep circling the block.
Jeffers, . . .

# Conjuring Roethke

Prickle a lamb,
giggle a yam,
beat a chrysanthemum
out of its head
with a red feather.
Dream of a pencil
or three airmail stamps
under your pillow.
Thank the good fairy
you're not dead.

The heat's on,
the window's gone,
the ceiling is sorry
it hurt you.
But this is not air
holding your hand,
nor weasels beneath
your dirt rug.
I think the corks
are out of breath,
the bottles begin
laughing a zoo.

I wish you were here.
The calendar is red,
a candle closes
the room.
If this is the life

we are all leaving
it's half as bad.
Hello again mad turnip.
Let's tango together
down to the clear
glad river.

## Fire Dance

In your eyes, I am a wealth of sin:
you see me with kegs of cognac,
harems of nubile lovers
bathing me in sweet-smelling oil.
You see me smoking opium
in the early hours, drowsy,

nibbling at a quail's wing
and a naked girl. O once in a while
I roll over and dictate a poem:
I smile graciously at this
charming act of condescension
and my thirty-three wives applaud

quietly. The next day it appears
in *The New Yorker* and I donate
the paltry reward to the veterans
of the Turko-Cuban Civil War
or the survivors of the Flemish
fire sale. Yes, Sister Michele,

it is all true: the fire dance
you are waiting for in the next
life happens every night
on my living room floor:
I writhe and read and write
until almost dawn until

there is not a light on
in the world and the ghosts
of beauty have disappeared
and my pride has crossed over
into complete shame and
emptiness and the thrush says
sleep you goddamned fool.

## Dear Reader

I am trying to pry open your casket
with this burning snowflake.

I'll give up my sleep for you.
This freezing sleet keeps coming down
and I can barely see.

If this trick works we can rub our hands
together, maybe

start a little fire
with our identification papers.

I don't know but I keep working, working

half hating you,
half eaten by the moon.

## No End to Fall River

No one has died for two hours.
How quietly the butterflies have taken over
Vermont. The peach tree is crying

canary, go home to the Virgin Islands
I don't need you you have been disloyal.
Adiós devil of rare delight

bleeding the night's arm
with onerous roil. Flapping
O carnivorous India ink

radish who are your favorite poets:
dropsical, dead or alive
remarks the fierce sink. Nasty

to bewail pestering boys . . .
Please detach this page and keep it.

# Bennington
*for Michael*

The rigadoon of verbena through
the sequined weather vanes!
I drove the dogsled into the morgue:
the stiffs bolted, frail comets
loped through the red night.

But there is only one poem,
why do I try to disguise that beautiful fact!
This year the poem is falling in love
not with itself for a change
but with innumerable swaggering bipeds,

with last night and today,
the scent of it, a lemon blossom.
From this house of hope I watch
a liquid sunset christen us,
children of a dying light; our innocence

is an old weapon, like a crossbow
our smiles of incomprehension.
You accepted the job at Bennington:
you are to be paid in rabbit skins.
I was down to my last donut

when I met the pastry magnate
from Peru: she had strange coiling fingers
and glazed eyes, but could waltz
fiendishly well. She had graduated
from Wellesley and Yale.

I don't want to dwell on this—
surely *you* understand the importance.
I can't do anything with my poem today.
See the chubby poet weeping!
I can't assassinate Bill Knott (1940–1966)

or Spiro T. Agnew, nor can I stand
on that chalky hill and gesture wildly at you
with a finished copy of it,
as if to say: look,
now we can screw in peace Cindy!

Cautiously approaching hysteria
the kit fox buries the last red grape in the snow.
Do not harm him. We will inhabit
the ghost towns slowly, hypnotizing
a mosquito, alone, endless drowning

in the mirror of a future kiss.
A white mouse lounging atop the alarm clock.
asks in her tinny pink voice,
"What are you writing now, smart-ass?"
I am probing the holes in the air.

The white elephant is trudging home
through the tantivy of snowflakes
after a long day at the ivory factory.
The white fish are yawning, envelopes
stuffed with snow in their holsters,

plastic bags over their shoulders.
And in the inkwell, a little mound,
maybe a gross of flakes, clutching
like a stadium of squids.
I am not afraid. My lack of fear

scares you, I know and I apologize.
The coins a man can earn at Bennington
these days by saying, "I think
your line-endings are fabulous Daphne."
You could never carry so many coins

home with you in a gunnysack,
though the last visiting bard
was caught buggering her right here
in the hallway. I have a bad back anyway
and that rich load would cripple me.

I have visited Bennington, Vermont
during one of those great blizzards.
I was a lonesome waif then,
one cracker in storage beneath
my ten-gallon hat. That was eight years ago.

Those girls possessed such admirable
maternal instincts! They kept me
from freezing in some very ingenious ways.
Their I.Q.'s were obviously above normal.
Nude as lampposts they'd skip

through the shifting landscape,
hands joined, hair whipping their crisp cheeks,
their delicious beavers accentuated
against the blinding brightness
of the moon's powdery blessing.

O falling asleep was not easy.
I understood nothing of their ways.
I was a smoldering volcano of desire!
So many years ago. Eighty-eight.
Through a liquid sunset

and a sequined weather vane
I drove the dogsled into the morgue.
On a chalky hill I stood and gestured
dumbly at you with a finished copy
of the only poem there is

I am writing now in a ghost town,
in a white nightgown, lounging atop
the soft alarm clock.
My lack of fear scares even me.
I fear the coins a man might earn,

ermine typewriter keys!
I have been in Bennington, Vermont
and seen the beavers gamboling
in the snowy, lemon-verbena moonlight.
Though I do not fully understand this blessing,

Michael, I give you mine.

# Carnegie Mellon
# Classic Contemporaries

Peter Balakian
*Sad Days of Light*

Marvin Bell
*The Escape into You*
*Stars Which See, Stars Which Do Not See*

Kelly Cherry
*Lovers and Agnostics*

Deborah Digges
*Vesper Sparrows*

Stephen Dobyns
*Black Dog, Red Dog*

Rita Dove
*Museum*
*The Yellow House on the Corner*

Stephen Dunn
*Full of Lust and Good Usage*
*Not Dancing*

Cornelius Eady
*Victims of the Latest Dance Craze*

Maria Flook
*Reckless Wedding*

Charles Fort
*The Town Clock Burning*

Tess Gallagher
*Instructions to the Double*

Brendan Galvin
*Early Returns*

Amy Gerstler
*Bitter Angel*

Colette Inez
*The Woman Who Loved Worms*

Denis Johnson
*The Incognito Lounge*

X. J. Kennedy
*Nude Descending a Staircase*

Greg Kuzma
*Good News*

Larry Levis
*The Dollmaker's Ghost*

Thomas Lux
*Sunday*
*Half Promised Land*

Jack Matthews
*An Almanac for Twilight*

David Mura
*After We Lost Our Way*

Carol Muske
*Skylight*

Gregory Orr
*Burning the Empty Nests*

Dave Smith
*The Fisherman's Whore*

Elizabeth Spires
*Swan's Island*

Maura Stanton
*Snow on Snow*
*Cries of Swimmers*

Gerald Stern
*Lucky Life*
*Two Long Poems*

James Tate
*Absences*
*The Oblivion Ha-Ha*

Jean Valentine
*Pilgrims*

Ellen Bryant Voigt
*The Forces of Plenty*

James Welch
*Riding the Earthboy 40*

Evan Zimroth
*Giselle Considers Her Future*